Stage 4

As wind and water remove soil from t[...]
they become less fertile in their turn.
Cattle move up the slopes
to graze, increasing the speed
of erosion.

Stage 5

When there is no longer enough grazing
land left to support cattle, sheep
and goats strip the land bare.

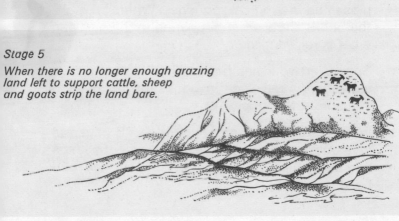

Stage 6

In the end hardly any soil is left,
and rocks can be seen.
Nothing can grow in the dust
which is left.
The land is a desert.

to teachers and parents

This is a LADYBIRD LEADER book, one of a series specially produced to meet the very real need for carefully planned *first information books* that instantly attract enquiring minds and stimulate reluctant readers.

The subject matter and vocabulary have been selected with expert assistance, and the brief and simple text is printed in large, clear type.

Children's questions are anticipated and facts presented in a logical sequence. Where possible, the books show what happened in the past and what is relevant today.

Special artwork has been commissioned to set a standard rarely seen in books for this reading age and at this price.

Full colour illustrations are on all 48 pages to give maximum impact and provide the extra enrichment that is the aim of all Ladybird Leaders.

A Ladybird Leader

deserts

by P. H. Armstrong

with illustrations by
Gerald Witcomb and Roger Hall

Ladybird Books Ltd Loughborough 1976

What deserts are

Deserts are parts of the world
that are very dry and hot.

They have less than 25 cm (10 ins)
of rain a year.

Sometimes no rain falls
for several years.
At Death Valley, California
and in the Sahara
the temperature has reached 60°C.

Where are the world's deserts ?

About one eighth of the land
in the world is desert.

The largest desert in the world
is the Sahara in North Africa.

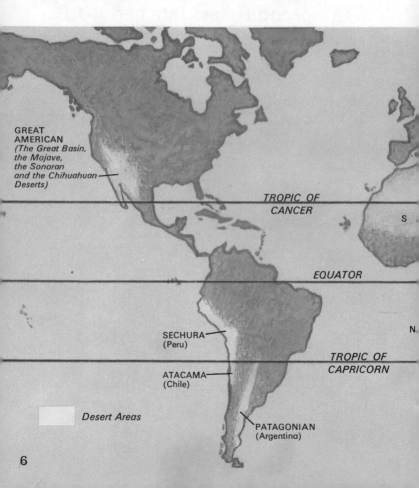

GREAT
AMERICAN
*(The Great Basin,
the Mojave,
the Sonoran
and the Chihuahuan
Deserts)*

*TROPIC OF
CANCER*

S

EQUATOR

N

SECHURA
(Peru)

*TROPIC OF
CAPRICORN*

ATACAMA
(Chile)

Desert Areas

PATAGONIAN
(Argentina)

Here too the hottest place on Earth is to be found.

The Sahara Desert covers an area nearly as large as that of the U S A.

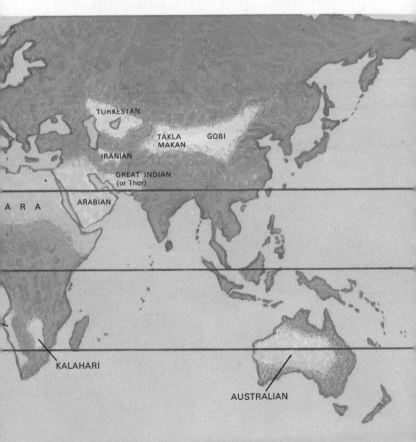

TURKESTAN

TAKLA MAKAN

GOBI

IRANIAN

GREAT INDIAN (or Thar)

A R A

ARABIAN

KALAHARI

AUSTRALIAN

Sandstorms

There are few plants
to cover the ground,
so sand and dust is blown about
by the wind.

In a sandstorm it may become
quite dark during the day.

When it is very hot
swirling 'dust-devils' or whirlwinds
sometimes form.
In these the winds
are often very strong.

Sandy deserts

Sometimes the sand is blown into dunes.

Crescent-shaped sand-dunes called *barchans* (say 'bar-kaans') are common in some deserts.

The Barchan dune is formed by the wind blowing in one direction

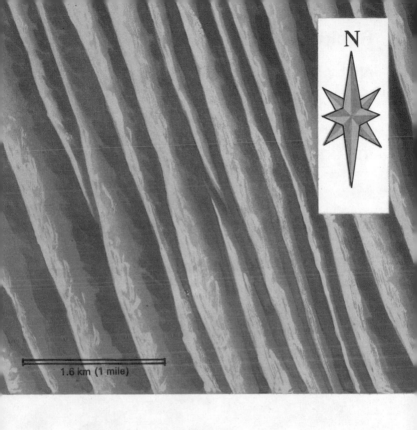

1.6 km (1 mile)

In Australia and parts of the Sahara many long, narrow dunes occur together.

These are called *seif* dunes.

Rocky deserts

Not all deserts are sandy.

Here is a rocky desert
in the Ahaggar Mountains
in Algeria.

13

The work of the wind

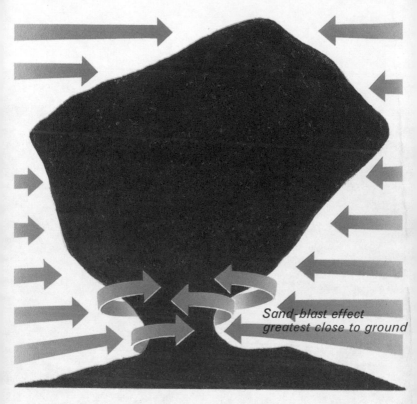

Sand-blast effect greatest close to ground

Sand blown by the wind
often carves rocks into strange shapes.

Those shown here
are called 'mushroom rocks'.

Since sand is too heavy
to be lifted far above the ground
the *erosion* (wearing away) of rock
is most rapid nearest the ground.

Water in the desert

When rain does come to deserts,
it comes in sudden storms.

A whole year's rainfall
may fall at one time.

Valleys which have been dry for years
may suddenly contain torrents
several metres deep.
Much soil is carried away
by the torrent.
This wears away the valley bed
which becomes deeper and deeper.

Oases

Sometimes in the middle of a desert
there are areas made fertile
by water from springs or wells.

These areas are called *oases*.

Crops such as date palms
may be grown in an oasis.

Plants that store water

Some desert plants have few leaves,
so very little water is lost to the air.

Cacti have fleshy stems
in which water is stored
for use in dry periods.

Barrel Cactus

Plants like this are called *succulents.*
Spines prevent animals
from eating the cacti
to obtain water.

Organ Pipe Cactus

Deep roots

Many desert plants
have roots that take water
from deep in the earth.

Roots of the Mesquite tree
in the American deserts
often reach a depth
of over 35 metres (over 38 yds).

Mesquite tree

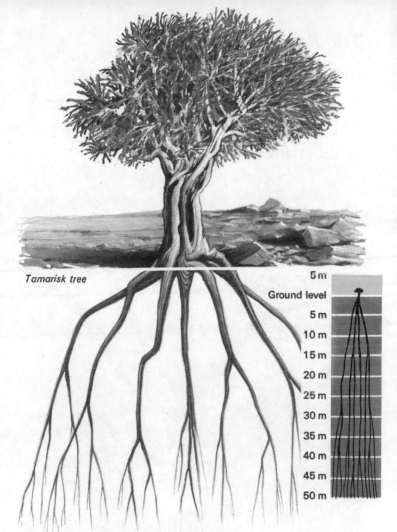

Tamarisk tree

5 m
Ground level
5 m
10 m
15 m
20 m
25 m
30 m
35 m
40 m
45 m
50 m

Those of the Tamarisk
have been traced down
to 50 metres (54.6 yds).

23

The deserts bloom

Some desert plants have seeds
that can lie for years in the dry soil
and yet grow into seedlings
when rain comes.

*A crocus-like bloom found mainly
in the northern Sahara*

White Desert Evening Primroses

Many flowers appear in the desert
after a rainstorm.

They grow from seeds, flower,
set their own seeds
and die in 6 - 8 weeks.

Camels

Camels store fat in their humps
so they can live without food
for many days.

They can also take in water
very quickly.

One camel drank over 100 litres (176 pints) of water in ten minutes, and then did not need to drink any more water for ten days.

Camels are still used for transport in some dry areas.

Lizards

Lizards are found
in almost all deserts.

Many are the same colour as sand
or stones and are hard to see.

In Australia there is a lizard
that can take in water
without drinking.

It absorbs water
like blotting paper.

*A Chuckwalla Lizard. This is the largest lizard
of North American deserts. It inflates its lungs
so that it cannot be removed from rock crevices.*

Fringe-toed Lizard

Some desert lizards burrow into sand
when it is very hot.

Kangaroo rats

These little animals
live in deserts in America.

They can live
without drinking any water at all.

They get all the water they need
from their food.

They look for food at night
and stay in their burrows
in the daytime.

Kangaroo rats lose very little water
from their skin
even when it is very, very hot.

They can jump as high as
2 metres (over 6 ft).

The Bushmen

Men have lived in some deserts
for a long time.

They know how to find food and water.

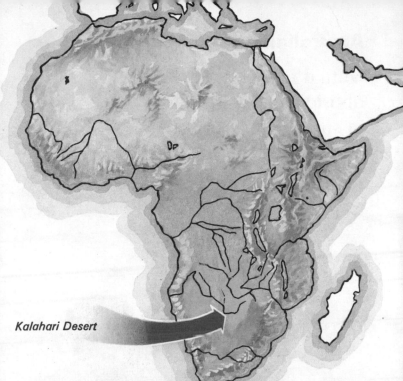

Kalahari Desert

The bushmen live
in the Kalahari Desert in Africa.

They hunt animals with spears
or bows and arrows
and eat berries and nuts.

Sometimes they have to carry water
over 20 km (over 12 miles)
in ostrich eggshells.

Australian aborigines

Until a few years ago
aborigines used to live
in small family groups
in the deserts of Australia.

A very large area was needed
to provide food for each person.

The aborigines moved
from place to place.

They dug up grubs and roots
and caught birds for food.

Now many aborigines work
on farms on the edge of the desert
or live in towns.

Bedouin

Some Arabs in the Near East
still live in tents.

They are called *bedouin*,
which means 'desert-dwellers'.

Their tents are made
of goat-hair cloth
stretched over poles.

They move from place to place
with their camels, sheep and goats.

The animals find food
where plants have grown after rain.

But now many bedouin
live in one place for most of the time.

Exploration

It is only in the last 150 years
that many deserts have been explored
by Europeans.

Many of these explorers
died of hunger, thirst
or from the great heat.

N
W   E
S

Weld Springs ✕

Mt Malcolm ✕
Mt Ida ✕   ✕ Mt Margaret
✕ Mt Leonora

Peake
Telegraph
Station

Lake Eyre

Brisbane

Geraldton

Perth

Port Augusta

Adelaide

Sydney
Canberra

Melbourne

TASMANIA

1869 ——————
1870 ——————
1874 ——————

Forrest's Expeditions

John Forrest between 1869 and 1874
explored much of the dry part
of Australia.

Mining

The earth under some deserts
contains minerals of great value.

For example, there is silver
in northern Mexico,
uranium in Utah and New Mexico,
and copper in Nevada
and the Atacama Desert.

Special towns are built for the miners.

Water has to be brought by pipe
for several hundred kilometres.

In the north-west of Australia
there are big iron ore mines.

The ore goes to the port by train.

Tom Price iron ore mine

Pilbara region

Desert area

41

Oil

Many of the world's biggest oilfields
lie under deserts.

The oilmen drill into the ground
to get the oil.

Oil is sometimes found as far down
as 3.2 km (2 miles).

The drill is held in place
by a drilling rig.

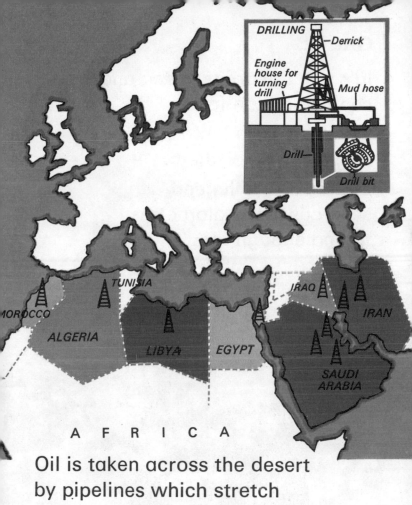

Oil is taken across the desert
by pipelines which stretch
over 1600 km (1,000 miles).

Nine million barrels of oil
flow every day
from wells in the world's deserts.

Grazing

In some dry areas sheep and cattle
can find a little food.

Wells are bored into the ground
to get water for them.

One animal will need
several square kilometres
to find enough food.

The farms need a great deal of land and are called 'ranches' in America and 'stations' in Australia.

Helicopters are used in some places to round up cattle because of the distances.

Farming the deserts

Good crops can often
be grown in deserts
if the land can be watered.

The water may have to be brought
a long way by canal.

In some places fresh water
is made out of sea water
and brought to the desert by pipeline.

*The All-American Canal takes much-needed water
from the river Colorado to the Imperial Valley
in the Sonoran Desert of California*

Sometimes the water
is sprayed onto the crops,
and sometimes it is brought
to the fields in little channels.

Irrigation

Bringing water to dry land
is called *irrigation*.

Here are pictures showing land
before and after irrigation.

Crops such as cotton now grow
where once there were
only a few bushes.

The amount of good farming land
in Israel, for example,
has been doubled by using irrigation.

Another use for deserts

Deserts are sometimes used for the launching of rockets.

There are very few people to be disturbed by the noise the rocket makes at blast-off.

If a rocket were to explode
there would be no one there
to be hurt.

*A Nike-Hercules missile lifting off
from White Sands Missile Range,
New Mexico*

Index